MW01132060

Dedicated to
R.J.A and V.C.D.

HOPE YOU ENJOY THIS BOOK
Karl Bailey 2021

My name is Karl Bailey Jr, I was born and raised in Austin, Texas. I grew up in a very creative household, with my two parents Karl and Christine with my only brother Robert. I've been into art since I was 3 years old and through years of developing my artistic talent, I've become very proficient even without a college degree.

After high school I didn't attend college. Instead, I taught myself graphic design software and combined with my art skills as a freelancer. Since 2001 I've created many dynamic designs for my clients, which contributed to my professional growth.

After I reached the milestone of turning 40 years old I reflected on my art career. Then I realized that all of my prior work was based on someone else's and helped them achieve their goals, but neglected to share my personal creative visions with the world.
So I decided to create my own characters and write a book that could be enjoyed worldwide for many generations.

This has been a very fulfilling experience to know that I can give the world a part of my creativity. But I must say that I'm most proud to inspire my two sons James and Josh to do more with their creative talent.
I also want to thank my lovely wife Rebecca for her love and support during this project.

Now that my first children's book is complete, I look forward to my next project, which is a comic graphic novel based on the same characters in this book but targeted for older youth.

RAINBOWS ALL AROUND US

Karl Bailey Jr

Hello my name is Candy the Crane. I want to tell you a story about my pals who learn about other types of rainbows besides the ones you see in the day sky.

Panic
The Panda

Ronda
The Red Panda

CoCo
The Koala

One day Panic and Ronda were out for a walk.

Then Ronda said,"Wow that rainbow is so beautiful!"

Panic asks her, "Did you know that there are other rainbows all around us?"
CoCo loves to fantasize about things he hears them saying.

There are even "rainbows" in the water called "Rainbow fish".
(real name: Boeseman's Rainbowfish)

CoCo imagines: A fairy princess defeating a water dragon which turns the fish into rainbows.

LEARNING ABOUT RAINBOW FISH

Boeseman Rainbow Fish(sounds like Bo-see-man) which are commonly found in the Ayamaru Lakes near West Papua, New Guinea.

This beautiful fish belongs to a fish family called Melanotaenia(sounds like Mel-a-no-teen-e-uh). Some rainbow fish can change their color based on mood, diet or change in location.

Rainbow fish get their flashy colors from cells called chromatosomes(sounds like crow-mat-o-some). They are also fresh water fish so they make great pets for kids at home.

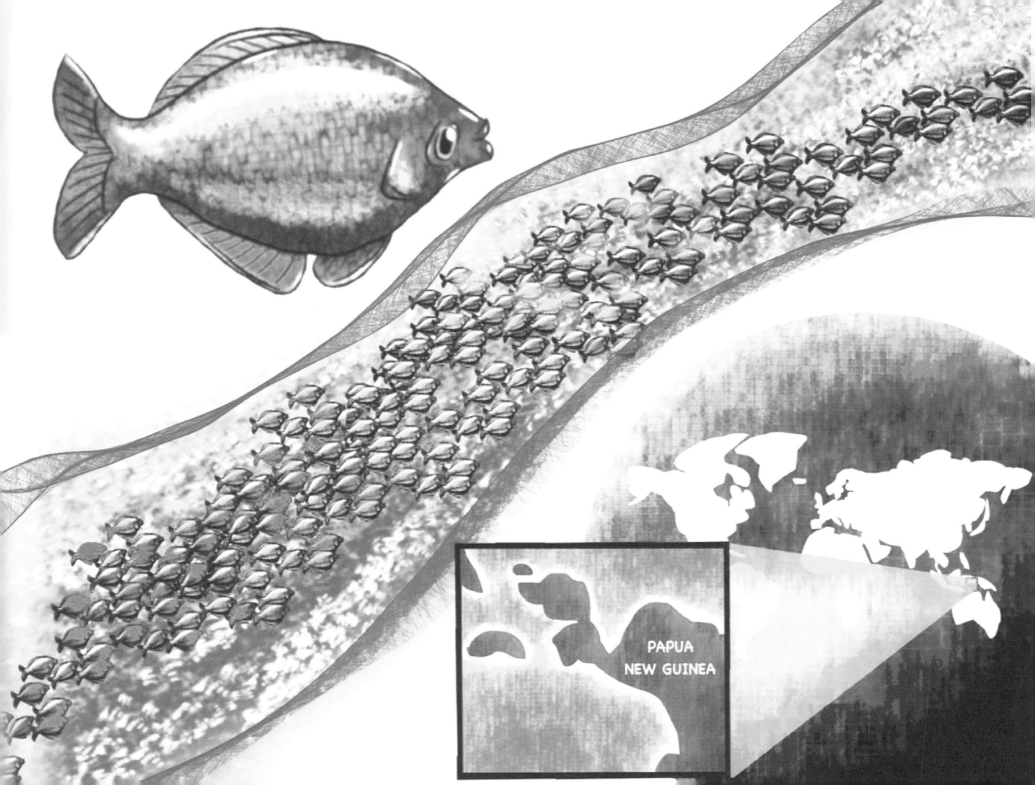

PAPUA
NEW GUINEA

"Another rainbow around us is in the colorful autumn leaves" says Panic.

CoCo imagines: A dragon who gets defeated by a swordsman in the forest which turns the trees colorful.

LEARNING ABOUT RAINBOW LEAVES

Normal green color leaves are green because of a pigment called Chlorophyll (sounds like clor-e-fill). Chlorophyll is a chemical that allows light to come into plants to help with it's growth and main functions for it's life. For most of the time we see only the green colors because it is covered up by the Chlorophyll except during the Autumn season as the weather gets cooler. Also the colder weather causes the leaves to seal off it's stalk trapping sugars inside and it may fall off the tree which is why we call this the Fall season.

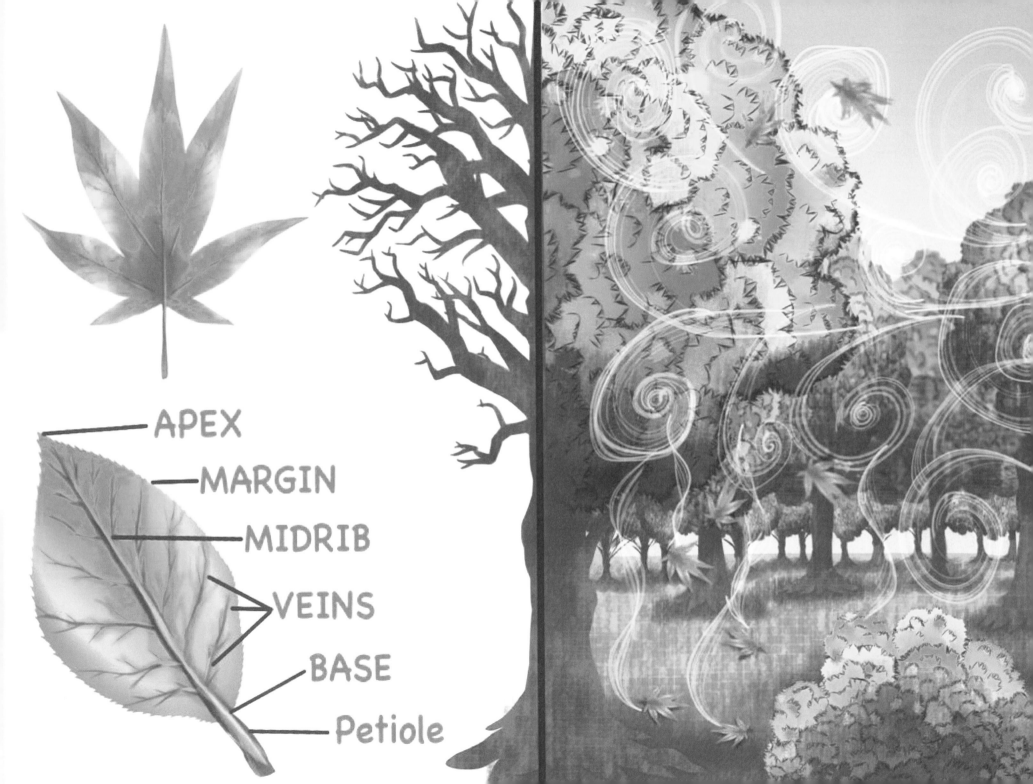

APEX

MARGIN

MIDRIB

VEINS

BASE

Petiole

We can even find rainbows in rocks called "Geode crystals" and caves called "Reed Flute Caves".

CoCo imagines: A Magical wizard who defeats a dragon in a cave and embeds colors all over the cave.

LEARNING ABOUT RAINBOWS IN ROCKS

Geodes crystal rocks are volcanic rocks with crystals formed inside by mineral deposits from Hydro-thermal fluids.

They are commonly found in the northern parts of the United States, Mexico, Brazil and in England they are called "potato stones".

Reed flute caves were named after a type of reed growing outside the cave located 790 feet below the earth's surface in Guilin Province, China.

The inside of this cave features magnificent stone pillars and stone structures which are formed by years of water flowing through it.

Actually, the rainbow color appearance is produced by multi-colored lights installed to enhance its magical effect.

CHINA

★GUILIN

REED FLUTE CAVES

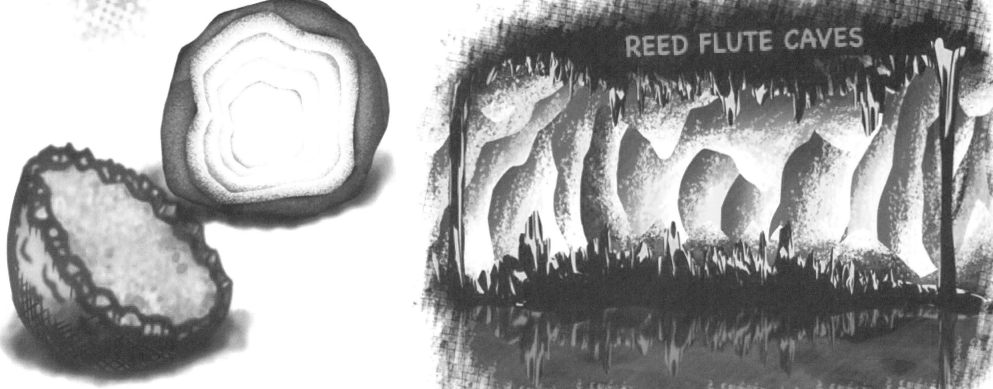

Later that evening, they witnessed one more rainbow in the night sky called "Aurora" or "Northern Lights".

CoCo imagines: A heroic archer defeating a dragon in the night sky causing colorful lights to stream out in the air.

LEARNING ABOUT NIGHT RAINBOWS

Aurora (sounds like uh-roar-uh) also known as "Northern lights" is a natural light show which can be seen in the highest areas in the Earth's Northern hemisphere and the North Pole.

Aurora is made when solar winds coming from the sun are pulled into the earth's northern and southern magnetic zones. The amount of each color can vary based on the amount of oxygen atoms, nitrogen molecules mixing with ultraviolet and infrared radiation.

No sighting is ever the same, it is truly a magical experience.

Aurora "Northern Lights"

SOLAR WINDS

NORTH POLE

SOLAR WINDS

MAGNETIC BORDER

SOUTH POLE

SOLAR WINDS

Ronda recalls what she just learned, then she shouts "Wow! It's true, there are other rainbows all around us!"

THE END

.........BUT WAIT, THERE'S MORE. TURN THE PAGE.

Hey kids, remember that these are just a few examples of different types of rainbows we see in nature, there's more to explore.

We hope this book inspires you all to learn more about God's big, beautiful world.

Reference links:

https://allthatsinteresting.com/why-leaves-change-color
https://sciencebob.com/why-do-leaves-change-color-in-the-fall/
https://en.m.wikipedia.org/wiki/Boeseman's_rainbowfish
https://www.fishkeepingworld.com/boesemani-rainbow/
https://geology.com/articles/geodes/
https://allthatsinteresting.com/reed-flute-cave
https://en.wikipedia.org/wiki/Aurora
https://blog.reedsy.com/standard-book-sizes/

COMING SOON

"Hey friends, don't miss my full dragon story in our upcoming comic graphic novel"

CPSIA information can be obtained
at www.ICGtesting.com
Printed in the USA
LVRC060547300321
682889LV00001B/3